About the Author

ARTHUR STECKLER was a cameraman in the U. S. Marine Corps, landing on Guadalcanal on what he calls "Opening Day." As a civilian he has worked as a director, production manager, and assistant director on all kinds of films, from *On the Waterfront* to TV commercials.

Mr. Steckler now divides his time between writing and making motion pictures. He and his wife and two daughters live in New London, Connecticut.

JAMES FLORA, the well-known illustrator and art director, has had his drawings published in many major U.S. magazines and has written and illustrated fifteen children's books as well.

Mr. Flora attended and later worked at the Cincinnati Art Academy, and after a stint as a mural painter, founded Little Man Press with Robert Lowry. Subsequently, he has been an art director, free-lance illustrator, and writer. Mr. Flora, his wife, and their five children now live in Rowayton, Connecticut.

nurse

nursery

palindrome

yanke

101 MORE WORDS
and how they began

Art

Jim

by
**Arthur
Steckler**

drawings by
**James
Flora**

goblin

pamplemousse

Doubleday & Company, Inc.
Garden City, New York

Library of Congress Cataloging in Publication Data

Steckler, Arthur.
  101 more words and how they began.

  SUMMARY: Traces the origins of 101 words.
  1. Language and languages—Etymology—Juvenile literature. (1.
English language—Etymology. 2. Language and languages—Etymology) I. Flora James. II. Title. P321.S7 428.1

Library of Congress Catalog Card Number 79-2397
ISBN: 0-385-15554-9 Trade
ISBN: 0-385-15555-7 Prebound
Text copyright © 1980 by Arthur Steckler
Illustrations copyright © 1980 by James Flora

THIS WAY TO THE EGRESS

There's a story about P. T. Barnum, who was a famous American showman, and one of the founders of what is now the Ringling Brothers and Barnum & Bailey Circus. Mr. Barnum's first circuses had sideshows of strange animals, freaks, and unusual acts. They were so popular that people didn't want to leave to let new customers in. So Mr. Barnum, it is said, had his sign painter make a very fancy sign which read: THIS WAY TO THE EGRESS! Well, the customers read the sign, went through a door to see the Egress, and found themselves out on the sidewalk. Although the sign read like an invitation to see one of his unusual and exotic birds or animals, Mr. Barnum was using an interesting word to suit his purpose, because the word "egress" is simply another word for "exit."

In music, which has a language of its own, a "crotchet" is a quarter note. Half a crotchet, or an eighth note, is a "quaver." Half a quaver, or a sixteenth note, is a "semiquaver." Half a semiquaver, or a thirty-second note, is a "demisemiquaver." And (if you're still there) half a demisemiquaver, or a sixty-fourth note, is a "hemidemisemiquaver," which sounds like something that would take longer to say than to play.

If you meant to say the word "butterfly," but you said "flutterby" instead, you would have made a "spoonerism," a word named after the Reverend William A. Spooner, who often interchanged the sounds of many words by accident. According to stories about him, the Reverend Spooner said things like "It is kistomary to cuss the bride." Even though butterflies "flutter by" more than they "butter flies," "flutterby" would still be considered a spoonerism.

Speaking of butterflies, if you followed one from England to France to Spain to Italy, its name would change from butterfly to *papillon* to *mariposa* to *farfalla* (and *you* would probably be very tired). The word butterfly in the French language is *papillon,* in Spanish it is *mariposa,* and in Italian it is *farfalla.* The same pretty insect with completely different names in four countries with four different languages.

While you were in France, if you ordered breakfast in a French restaurant and asked for *pamplemousse jus,* you might not know what sort of strange thing would appear. In fact, you could be disappointed to find that it was only grapefruit juice, because even though a *pamplemousse* sounds as though

I'LL HAVE PAMPLEMOU JUS

OUI, MONSIEUR

it might be a huge, trampling animal, it's simply the French word for grapefruit, and *jus,* if you hadn't already guessed it, is the French word for juice.

If you take the word "sleep" and the word "over" and arrange them one way, you have "sleep over." Arrange them the other way and you have "oversleep." There's quite a bit of difference between "sleeping over" and "oversleeping."

Another word for evening might be night, and yet an evening gown and a nightgown are certainly quite different. You probably wouldn't wear an evening gown to bed any more than you'd wear a nightgown to a party, unless it was a party where you were sleeping over.

If someone entered the room while you were playing Ping-Pong, and heard the sound the ball made—ping-pong, ping-pong—that person might be able to guess the name of the game even if he had never heard it before. That's because the word Ping-Pong is echoic or onomatopoeic, and means a word formed to imitate a sound. There are many, many echoic words we use in our language: clash, crash, smash, bash,

splash, sizzle, fizzle, and a big, long word, "tintinnabulation," which means the tinkling sound of bells and came from the tinkling sound of bells.

Just as there are new words which enter our language all the time, there are old words which pass out of general use and become obsolete, which means out-of-date. The word "batlet," for example, meant a wooden mallet used by laundresses for beating clothes. As people stopped using mallets to beat clothes, they also stopped using the word for that mallet. So the word batlet became obsolete, probably to be replaced by a word for a more modern way of washing clothes. Languages are constantly changing as new words enter common usage and old words go out of style and are no longer used.

So it's easy to see how words can confuse us, amuse us, tease us, and please us. There are words like outlaw and inlaw, horse race and racehorse, shotgun and gunshot. There are words that come from people and places and initials. There are words like pipkin and grivet and flibbertigibbet, lobster and mobster, and flivver and trivet.

There are words whose origins are not too difficult to figure out, like popcorn, breakfast, pancake, kneepad, and scarecrow. But there are hundreds of words whose origins are strange or interesting or humorous. Here are just a few.

Words About Ourselves

smile

It might be nice to start these 101 words with a SMILE, but some people might prefer to start them with a smirk. Yet both SMILE and smirk come from the same source and are closely related. The Anglo-Saxon word "smercian," after entering several European languages, became smirk, while the Old English word "smearcian" became SMILE.

dimple

Sometimes where there's a smile there's a DIMPLE. A DIMPLE was once a "dumpfel" in the German language, a "dompelen" in the Dutch language, and a "dimpul" in Middle English, and meant "a deep pool or a deep hole in water," which seems like a strange thing to find on a face.

tooth

Other times where there's a smile, there's a TOOTH, or a whole mouthful of teeth. The word TOOTH came from "tothe" and "tanth" and "tand" and "zand" and "dent." It came from the Middle English and Teutonic and Dutch and Old High German and Latin languages. Along the way "dent" gave us the word dentist, a person who helps us take good care of our teeth.

molars

Most people have an assortment of teeth, including some called MOLARS. MOLARS get their name from the Latin "molaris" and "mola", which mean millstone and mill. Mill-stones are used to grind grains in mills; MOLARS are used to grind foods. So it seems perfectly logical for MOLARS to have taken their name from mills and millstones.

cavity

While examining your molars or other teeth, your dentist may find a CAVITY. A CAVITY may come from too many sweets, but the *word* CAVITY comes from the Latin "cauus" and Medieval Latin "cavitas," meaning hollow. CAVITY is from the same word family that gives us the words cave and excavate. If you have a CAVITY that feels like a cave and seems to need excavating, maybe you'd better see your dentist.

drill

Where you find a cavity, you usually will find the need for a DRILL. The word DRILL comes from the Dutch words "drillen" and "dril," meaning a hole. It is related to the Middle English word "thirl" and "tril," as in "nostril" or "nose-tril," which of course is an opening in the nose. It is felt that the word thrill might be related to DRILL, although most patients don't get a thrill from the dentist's DRILL.

nozzle

Continuing this imaginary trip to the dentist even further, when it's time to drill the cavity in your tooth, the dentist will use a NOZZLE to spray water or air at the cavity. The word NOZZLE means little nose, and comes from the English "nozle." When someone starts to stick his little nose into your mouth while the dentist is drilling your cavity, it's time to go on to some other words.

sideburns

Most people know the word for the long side-whiskers some men grow. They are called SIDEBURNS, of course, and got their name from General Burnside, a famous Union general in the Civil War. Because General Burnside wore SIDE-BURNS, his soldiers and other people started calling side-whiskers "burnsides," which somehow got reversed and became SIDEBURNS, and that is what they're called today.

11

Words About Things We Enjoy

seesaw

If you have ever watched a person sawing wood, you may have noticed that the movement of the saw looked like the movement of a SEESAW in a playground. It was the motion of the saw over and over again and the sound "see-saw-see-saw" that suggested the word SEESAW to someone long ago. That person had invented a word which would be accepted in the English language, and probably didn't even know it.

trampoline

Sometimes in a playground or gymnasium we will see a TRAMPOLINE, a device which seems to have taken its name from the Italian word "trampolo" meaning stilt, and "trampoli" meaning stilts. When we watch how performers on a TRAMPOLINE seem suspended in midair, it sometimes appears that they are supported by stilts.

tennis

Imagine playing a game in which the other player hit the ball to you and called out "Take that!" It doesn't sound very sporting, but some people think that is how we got the name for the game of TENNIS. The Latin word "tenere," which meant to take, led to the French "tenez," and the Middle English "tenetz," which meant "receive the ball!" or "take that!"

marathon

When we think of a long-distance race or a dance contest, we often think of the word MARATHON. But why was a long-distance race named after a village 20 miles from Athens, Greece? Well, almost 2,500 years ago on a plain near the village of MARATHON, a great battle was fought between the Athenians and Persians. When the Athenians won the battle, a Greek runner was sent the 20 miles to announce the victory, after which he dropped dead, according to legend. Officially, a MARATHON race is now 26 miles, 385 yards

I'M VACATING MY HOME

long, but the word has come to mean any long and difficult race or contest. MARATHON has even given us words like tele-thon, bike-athon, swim-athon, and walk-athon, whether we like it or not.

vacation

If you saw the words: vacant, void, and wasted used to describe your VACATION, you'd think you probably had a terrible time. Yet those words are all related to the word VACATION, which comes from the Latin words "vacare" and "vacatio" and the Middle English "vacacioun." When we vacate something, we leave it empty or unoccupied. By vacating our school or office, we are taking a VACATION, even if it's vacant, void, and wasted!

picnic

One activity many people enjoy on vacation is a PICNIC, a word that was formed by a reduplication, or repeating of a syllable. The French words "piquer," meaning to pick, and "nique," meaning a trifle or morsel, led to the French "pi-quenique," which eventually became the English PICNIC.

kite

After you've enjoyed your picnic during your vacation, you might want to fly a KITE, which seems quite harmless. Yet the KITE you fly at the end of a string was named for a ferocious hawk because of the similar flying movements of the toy and the actual bird. The Anglo-Saxon word "cyta," the Middle English word "kite," and the Breton word "kidel" were all words for hawk, which eventually gave the name KITE to that popular toy.

ukulele

Most people enjoy music, and one instrument that's quite popular is the Hawaiian UKU-LELE. It looks like a small guitar, and is played by moving the fingers very quickly over the strings, which is how it got its name. In the Hawaiian language, the word "uku" means flea or insect; the word "lele" means to jump or fly. Put them together and you have UKULELE, or jumping flea, which is how the fingers seem to move on the strings and is a very colorful name for a musical instrument.

saxophone

Another musical instrument, the SAXOPHONE, was named for the man who invented it, Mr. Adolphe Sax. After he invented the instrument in 1840, Mr. Sax named it by adding the Greek work "phone," meaning sound, to his name, Sax. Mr. Sax's name was also given to the saxtuba and saxhorn, two other instruments he invented which never became quite as well known as his SAXOPHONE.

bugle

A musical instrument that people sometimes enjoy, and sometimes don't, is the BUGLE. Usually played to wake up sleeping campers at summer camp and soldiers at military bases, BUGLES have become a kind of musical alarm clock. In the Old French language, the word BUGLE means a wild ox, and comes from the Latin "buculus," which means a young ox. Once known as a bugle horn, possibly meaning the horn of an ox, the word has since been shortened to (the sometimes popular, sometimes not) BUGLE.

piccolo

Most people know that a PICCOLO is a "small" musical instrument, but some people might not know that the word PICCOLO actually means small. In the Italian language, the word for small is PICCOLO, and the definition of PICCOLO is small or petty. People who play the PICCOLO are known as piccoloists, and can be small or large, as they choose.

guitar

Seated near the piccolo player might be a musician playing a GUITAR, an instrument that has a long word history. Starting as the Greek "kithara," it became the Latin "cithara," a lute or lyre, which preceded an instrument called the zither, another word from "cithara." It then became known as the Arabic "qitara," the Spanish "guitarra," and the French "guitare" before becoming the instrument and word we know today, the GUITAR.

fiddle

To complete this strange orchestra, we come to the word FIDDLE. Even though it's a violin or a member of the viol family, to many people the FIDDLE has become the humorous word for a violin. We never hear of a FIDDLE concerto, yet we often hear of someone "fiddling around." The word FIDDLE started as the Latin "vitula," became the Medieval Latin "vidula," then became the Middle English and Anglo-Saxon "fithele" before becoming the word FIDDLE. The same people who thought FIDDLE was humorous must have thought of fiddle-dee-dee, fiddle-faddle, and fiddlesticks in a similar way since they all mean "nonsense" today.

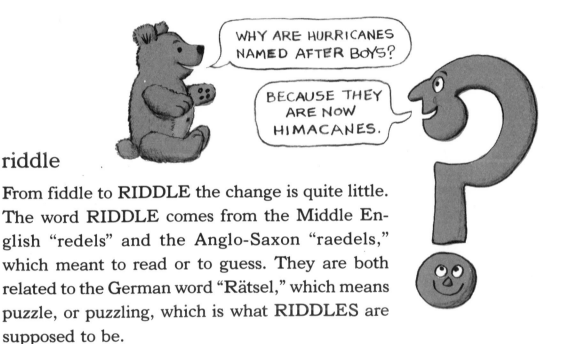

WHY ARE HURRICANES NAMED AFTER BOYS?

BECAUSE THEY ARE NOW HIMACANES.

riddle

From fiddle to RIDDLE the change is quite little. The word RIDDLE comes from the Middle English "redels" and the Anglo-Saxon "raedels," which meant to read or to guess. They are both related to the German word "Rätsel," which means puzzle, or puzzling, which is what RIDDLES are supposed to be.

teddy bear

One word that is used quite often was named for a man, President Theodore Roosevelt. President Roosevelt was very fond of hunting large animals such as lions, tigers, and bears. Since the nickname for Theodore is Teddy, and many people referred to President Roosevelt by that name, it was not surprising that someone would make a stuffed toy bear and call it a TEDDY BEAR. President Roosevelt would probably be amazed if he knew how many TEDDY BEARS there are around the world, all named after him.

Words About Things We Eat and Drin

lunch

If you sat down to have LUNCH and someone served you a large "lump" of bread, you might be a little surprised. Yet you might be just as surprised to know that LUNCH originally meant a lump of bread. The light meal known as LUNCH led to the more formal meal known as luncheon, and the place to have those meals, a luncheonette.

celery

Some people might enjoy a stalk of CELERY with their lunch, while others prefer a sprig of parsley. Yet by examining the word CELERY we find it means parsley. The Greek and Latin word "selinon" became the Italian "selini," which in turn became the French "celeri," all of which meant "a kind of parsley."

salad

If you make a SALAD and people complain that it's too salty, tell them that's what the word means. SALAD comes from the Latin word "sal" and the Italian "sale," both meaning salt. They led to the Provençal "salada," the Old French "salade," and the Middle English "salat" and SALAD, meaning salted or pickled vegetables. The words salary, sausage, and sauce are all related to the word SALAD.

mayonnaise

Sometimes when we serve a salad we serve it with MAYONNAISE, a word believed to have originated in the town of Mahón on the island of Minorca in the Mediterranean Sea. According to legend, there was once a shortage of milk and cream on the island, which prevented a chef from making his usual sauce. Being a clever chef, he invented a sauce without milk or cream, using eggs, oil, and vinegar instead. Evidently the sauce was quite good, and was named Sauce Mahónnaise in honor of the town of Mahón. From Mahonnaise to MAYONNAISE was a simple change.

YOU'RE A GOOD-LOOKING KID

noodle

In slang, using your NOODLE means using your head, but in food, using your NOODLE means using your macaroni or dumpling. Even though the NOODLES we eat may come from anywhere, that word NOODLE comes from the German "Nudel," meaning macaroni, and the German "Knödel," meaning dumpling. The other word NOODLE comes from "noddy," meaning a fool, and "noddle," meaning the head, and has nothing to do with the NOODLE we eat.

cider

The CIDER we sometimes drink with a meal was named for a much stronger drink. Originally a fermented liquor made from apples, cherries, or other fruits, it was called "shekar" in the Hebrew language. Shekar became the Greek "sikera," the Latin "sicera," then the Old French "sidere" and "cidere." The meaning of the early words for CIDER was simply "strong drink," a meaning which changed as the word changed.

soda

When we ask for a SODA with our meal, we are asking for something "firm, solid, and hard," as strange as that may seem. The word SODA comes from the Latin word "solidus," meaning solid, and the Italian "sodo," meaning firm. There are many meanings for the word SODA other than the beverage we drink. The Middle Latin SODA meant headache, and the word SODA in chemistry refers to different salts of sodium and baking SODA. With all the different meanings of the word SODA, be sure to ask for the right one the next time you're thirsty.

tapioca

For dessert you may want to try some TAPIOCA pudding. The word TAPIOCA comes from an obscure Brazilian language known as Tupi, and is actually formed by three smaller words: "ty" which means juice, "pya" which means heart, and "oc" which means to squeeze out. Put them all together and you have "typyaoc," the Tupi word meaning to squeeze out the juice and heart of the root of the cassava plant.

marshmallow

If tapioca seems too complicated, let's try MARSHMALLOW. A marsh mallow is one of the plants of the mallow family, which grows in marshes. The root of this plant is used to make medicine as well as the soft candy we all know. MARSHMALLOW takes its name from the Old English "merscmealwe."

tutti frutti

If marshmallow still sounds complicated, we have one more dessert, TUTTI FRUTTI, that's not complicated at all. Tutti comes from the Italian language and means total or all. Frutti is also an Italian word and means fruit, as if you didn't know. Put them together and you have "all fruits," which is supposed to be the flavor of TUTTI FRUTTI ice cream, candy, and chewing gum.

Words About Things We Wear

diaper

When we were very young, we probably wore DIAPERS to keep us clean and dry. Yet the word DIAPER originally meant a fine, valuable, ornamented cloth, often used as a table cloth or napkin. It came to us from the French, Latin, and Greek languages. From "diaspros" to "diasprus" to "di-apré" it became DIAPER, something we usually don't use to set the table.

jacket

When we put on a JACKET, we probably don't think of it as a coat of mail, which is what medieval soldiers wore hundreds of years ago. And yet, that is how we got the word JACKET. In France, the most common male name is Jacques, which became the name for the coat of mail or sleeveless leather coat that most men wore at that time. The name Jacques was given the diminutive Jaquette, which means something smaller than the original. As the word jaquette became JACKET, the meaning changed from a soldier's coat to the short coat we all know and wear, and even came to mean the covering for a book and the outer skin of a potato.

zipper

Sometimes the jacket we wear will have a slide fastener or ZIPPER to help keep it closed. Whenever we open or close the ZIPPER, it goes "zip," or at least it should, which is how it got its name. ZIPPER is one of the best examples of echoic words, words formed by the sound of the action involved.

suede

It's possible that the jacket we wear might be made of SUEDE. Whether the SUEDE came from Kalamazoo or Timbuktu, we should know that the word came from Sweden. The French name for Sweden is SUEDE, which gave the name "gants de Suède," meaning gloves of Sweden, to Swedish gloves many years ago. Although the gloves and leather are now made in other countries, the word for that soft leather remains SUEDE, the French name for Sweden.

gloves

Speaking of GLOVES, that was once the word for the palms of the hands, which seems appropriate. The Gothic word "lofa" meant flat hand or palm of the hand. That led to the Germanic "galofa," the Old Norse "glofi," the Anglo-Saxon "glof," meaning paw, the Middle English "glofe," and eventually to the word we now use, GLOVE.

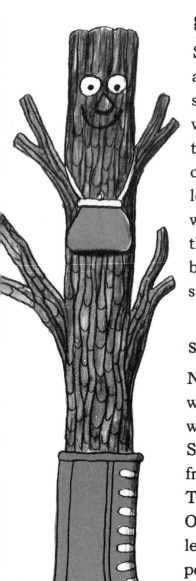

galoshes

Since your hands are protected by gloves, how about something to protect your feet, like the overshoes known as GALOSHES? Well, GALOSHES weren't always high, rubber overshoes. Originally they were wooden shoes, or the wooden forms called shoemakers' lasts, and were known as "kalopous" in the Greek language. "Kalon" means wood and "pous" means the foot in Greek. Then they were given the French name "galoches" which became our word GALOSHES, and are almost sure to keep your feet warm and dry.

scarf

Now that your hands and feet are warm, you should wrap a wallet around your neck to keep your neck warm. But a wallet shouldn't go around the neck; a SCARF should. And yet the word SCARF comes from the Old Norse "skreppa," meaning wallet. That came from the Old French "escreppe," and Old Norman French "escarpe," which meant wallet, or "pilgrim's wallet," which was a purse suspended from the neck.

saddle

Although *people* may not wear SADDLES, horses and some other four-legged animals do. It may not be very surprising to find that the word SADDLE comes from the words "to sit." This "seat" is found in many languages, Middle English "sadel," Anglo-Saxon "sadol," German "Sattel," Celtic "sadell," and in the languages of most countries where SADDLES were used.

24

blanket

Somebody once said that he liked any color horse as long as it was brown. It might also be said that he liked any color horse BLANKET as long as it was white, because white, or blank, is where the word BLANKET comes from. The French word "blanquette" is the diminutive of the French word "blanc," meaning white or blank. From blanquette to BLANKET was a simple change.

mask

Every so often, we may see a horseman galloping across our TV screen wearing a MASK. Some people might think he looks "ridiculous" or like a "fool" or "buffoon." Yet that's where the word MASK comes from. The Arabic word "maskharat," which meant ridiculous or a jester, became the Italian "mascara," meaning a MASK, which is what jesters used to wear. "Mascara" became the word for the makeup that some women apply to their eyelashes, and eventually became the French word "masque," a shortened form of "masquerade," and a party where people often wear MASKS.

Words About Things We Use

apron

After a meal is over, someone often puts on an APRON and helps clear things away. Yet it might be surprising to find that an apron was once called "a napron." APRON started out as the Latin word "mappa" which meant a cloth or table napkin. Then it became "naperon" in the Old French language, after which it entered the Middle English language as "napron." Then, because someone separated the word incorrectly, "a napron" became "an APRON," and it's remained that way ever since.

tweezers

Another word we use quite often which went through many changes over the years is the word TWEEZERS. In France, long ago, a surgeon's case of instruments was called an "étui." It contained scissors, knives, and other surgical items. These "étuis" became "etwees" which became "twees" which became "tweezes" which eventually became TWEEZERS.

camera

The next time you use a CAMERA, it might surprise you to find that you are using a room or chamber. The Latin word CAMERA meant a vault or room, and that meaning was adapted to our photographic CAMERAS, since there is a dark little chamber between the lens and the film.

film

When we use a camera, it should be loaded with FILM, yet the word FILM means a thin skin or membrane. FILM came from the Middle English "fel," the Dutch "vel," the Gothic "fill," and the Anglo-Saxon "filmen," meaning membrane or skin. Considering how thin and flexible photographic FILM must be, it's easy to see how it got its name from thin skin or membrane.

button

Now, if you're ready to take a picture, all you have to do is press the little bud, or BUT-TON. The Old French word "boton" and the Middle English  "bouton" meant bud, which later came to mean BUTTON, and referred to a pushed-out knob, whether on a camera, a jacket or anyplace else. BUTTON and bud are related to the French word "boutonnière," which is a flower worn in the buttonhole of a jacket lapel.

crayon

Another way to make a picture is to take a CRAYON and draw one, but tracing the origin of the word CRAYON will first take us to the island of Crete in the Mediterranean Sea. A chalky white substance was found on Crete, and was given the Latin name "creta."

This chalk entered the French language as "craie," later becoming CRAYON. Even though CRAYON is the word for the waxy drawing material we all know, it is also the French word for pencil.

mirror

Now that you've made a lovely picture with your camera or your crayon, hold it up to a MIRROR and behold a miracle, for that's how the word MIRROR began. The Latin word "mirari" and the Old French and Middle English "mirour" meant to admire or wonder at, and are related to the words miracle, mirage, marvelous, and of course, MIRROR.

kaleidoscope

Another way to see beautiful forms would be to look through a KALEIDO-SCOPE, and that's exactly what the word means. The Greek word "kalos" means beautiful, "eidos" means form, and "skopeo" means to see. Put them together and you have "kaloseidos-skopea," or KALEIDOSCOPE, the toy that lets you see beautiful forms.

decalcomania

Another long word for something we use to see a picture or design is DECALCOMANIA, or decal for short. Many people use decals on windows and other surfaces. DE-CALCOMANIA comes from two words, the French word "décalquer," meaning to counterdraw or countertrace, and

28

the Greek word "mania," meaning madness. We can assume that when DECALCOMANIAS were first devised, people showed a certain madness in transferring pictures and designs all over the place.

easel

With all the pictures we've been talking about, it might be nice to find an EASEL to place them on. It should be something that will stand very still and be quite strong, like a beast of burden. That's exactly how EASEL got its name, from the German word "Esel" and the Dutch word "ezel," which mean ass or donkey. They usually stand very still, are quite strong, and are certainly beasts of burden.

Words About People

chef

When we think of someone who prepares fine food, we often think of a French CHEF; not just any French CHEF, but the chief CHEF, or the head CHEF. Yet in the French language, CHEF means chief, and both CHEF and chief come from the Latin word for head, which is "caput." We might say that a CHEF is the chief or head cook.

nurse

As we know, NURSES help to take care of people and also make sure they get proper nourishment, and it's from "nourishment" and "to nourish" that we get the word NURSE. The Latin words "nutricius," "nutrix" and "nutrire" meant nurse, to feed, and to nourish. They led to the Old French "norice" and "nurrice," which became the Middle English "norice" and "nurice," meaning nurse or governess. From NURSE we get the word nursery. Nurseries are places where young children or trees are taken care of and provided with proper nourishment.

Eskimo

Speaking of nourishment, most people know that ESKIMOS eat their meat raw, but they may not know that's what the word **ESKIMO** means. In the American Indian languages, **ESKIMO** is spelled "eskimantik," "askimowew," and "askkimey," and means "eaters of raw flesh."

Yankee

The word **YANKEE** seems to have all kinds of meanings. During the Civil War, Northerners were called **YANKEES** by Southerners, yet in the First World War, both Southerners and Northerners were called **YANKEES** by the English. Americans refer to New Englanders as **YANKEES**, yet the New York **YANKEE** baseball team is not a New England team. The word **YANKEE** goes back to Revolutionary War days and the song "Yankee Doodle," which **YANKEES** evidently "tootled" on their fifes while marching. **YANKEE** is thought by some people to be a combination of the Dutch words "Jan," for John, and "kees," for cheese, resulting in the strange name John Cheese. Others feel that Janke, which is the nickname for the Dutch name Jan, gave us the word **YANKEE**.

wizard

People who are very good at what they do are often called **WIZARDS**. Although the word **WIZARD** is related to the words "wit" and "wise," it came to mean a magician or sorcerer. The Old Norse "viskr" and Icelandic "visk-r" meant clever or wise, and were adapted to the Old French "guisart" and the Middle English "wisard," which later became **WIZARD**, a clever and wise person who might be a magician, a sorcerer, a nurse, or a chef.

goblins

Somehow when we think of wizards we think of GOBLINS. GOBLINS are mischievous spirits. In the Greek language, "kobalos" meant sprite, which is an elf, fairy, or pixie. The Old French and Middle English "gobelin," meaning evil or mischievous spirit, came from the Medieval Latin "gobelinus," which meant a goblin or "a household god." If your household has GOBLINS, you'd better call an exterminator or wizard.

skeleton

Speaking of wizards and goblins reminds us of SKELETONS. Although SKELETONS aren't people now, some of them were before. The Greeek word "skleros," meaning dry or hard, and the Greek "skeletos," meaning dried up, like a mummy, became SKELETON, which originally meant a dried-up mummy. Next Halloween when a SKELETON comes to your door for trick or treat, remember that it started out as a mummy.

gypsy

Have you ever tried to figure out where the word GYPSY began? If you guess that it came from the word Egyptian, your guess is correct, but is based on an error. The word GYPSY is from the Middle English "gyptian," short for Egyptian, since GYPSIES were believed to have come from

Egypt. But they originally came from India, with only a stopover in Egypt, and brought us the name GYPSY, a word error which entered our language and stayed.

jack-o'-lantern

With Halloween just about over, the only face still at your door is probably the grinning face on the pumpkin, or JACK-O'-LANTERN. The nickname for the name John is Jack, and becomes a common name for males. The lantern, of course, refers to the Halloween pumpkin which is usually lighted with a candle. So, a JACK-O'-LANTERN simply means the face on the pumpkin, or the man of the lantern.

ghost

About the only person, or thing, that hasn't come to your door so far is a GHOST. But GHOST has had so many spellings and pronunciations that the poor thing doesn't know what to do. Starting out as the Indo-European "gheiz," related to the German "Geist," it changed to the Dutch "geest," the Anglo-Saxon "gast," the Old Saxon "gest," the Middle English "gost" or "goost." Then it is thought that a printer's error gave it the name GHOST, which is what it remains today. All those spellings meant a terrifying spirit or an angry demon, probably because nobody ever got its name right.

Words About Places on the Map

equator

Although the EQUATOR is not actually a place on the map, it is an imaginary line around the earth which divides the earth's surface into the northern and southern hemispheres. It divides it in equal halves, and it is from the word equal that we get the word EQUATOR. The Latin words "aequus" and "aequare," meaning equal or even, led to the Middle English and Lower Latin "aequator," which became our word EQUATOR, something a young student once defined as a "menagerie lion running around the middle of the Earth."

Sahara

Just north of the equator in Africa is the largest desert on earth, the SAHARA Desert. Over 3 million square miles in size, it might be described as a desert-desert, and that's exactly what its name means. In the Arabic language the word for desert is "sahra," which is where we get the name SAHARA. When we say SAHARA Desert, we are really saying desert-desert, as most Arabs will tell you.

Nevada

One of the United States which also has deserts, and some snow, is the state of NEVADA, and it is from the snow that

NEVADA takes its name. The Latin words "nix" and "nivis," meaning snow, led to the Middle Latin "nivatus," which became the Spanish "nevado" and eventually the name NE-VADA, a land of snow and desert.

Vermont

Is there a state known for green mountains? Of course there is: the state of VERMONT, which actually means green mountain. It takes its name from the French words "vert," meaning green, and "mont," meaning mount or mountain. Since VERMONT means green mountain, it seems quite appropriate

that it is known as the Green Mountain State, and has a mountain range known as the Green Mountains.

Canada

Bordering Vermont on the north is CANADA. According to legend, when early explorers first came to CANADA, they asked the Indians the name of the place. The Indians, thinking they were asking the name for the huts whch made up their village, gave them the name "canata." From "canata" and "canada," the American Indian words for huts, came the name for the nation of CANADA.

HELLO, GOOD-LOOKING

Wisconsin

Just south of Canada lies the state of WISCONSIN. The Ojibwa Indians, or Chippewas, lived in the area now known as WISCONSIN. They named the area "wishkonsing," their term for "the muskrat's or beaver's hole," and meant the Wisconsin River in the state which is now WISCONSIN.

Chicago

Another American place which takes its name from an American Indian language is the city of CHICAGO. Possibly from the same tribe that named Wisconsin, the Ojibwas, came the Indian term "she-kag-ong," which meant "the wild-onion place," and of course became the name CHICAGO, a city which is known today for much more than wild onions.

Oklahoma

Traveling southwest from Chicago, we come to OKLAHOMA, known as a land of American Indians, especially of the Choctaw tribe. Since "okla" means people and "humma" means red in the Choctaw language, it is easy to see how we get the name OKLAHOMA, land of the red people.

Florida

FLORIDA was given its name by Juan Ponce de Léon, who discovered it in April 1513, during the Eastertime Feast of Flowers or Pascua Florida, as it is called in Spanish. Ponce de Léon was right in naming FLORIDA for its flowers.

moon

The last place on our map is the MOON, which may not be on a world map but will certainly be on a map of our solar system. In astronomy, a month is measured by the revolution of the MOON around the earth. The Greek words "mene" meaning MOON, "men" meaning month as measured by the MOON, and the Gothic word "mena" led to the Anglo-Saxon "mona," which in turn led to the Middle English "mone" and the English word MOON.

Words About the Animal World

bumblebee

It's easy to know when a BUMBLEBEE is near you because it's the insect that hums. You may ask why it wasn't called a "humblebee," and the answer is, it was, originally. The first part of the word humblebee is echoic, of course, from the sound of the bee, and comes from the Middle Dutch "hummel" and the Middle English "humbel-bee." The change from humblebee to BUMBLEBEE probably came from children changing humming to buzzing, and therefore humblebee to BUMBLEBEE.

beetle

Another little insect that might just bite is the BEETLE, which means "the biting one." The Anglo-Saxon words "bitan," "bitela," and "bitel" led to the Middle English "betil" and the English BEETLE, all of which meant to bite. There are over 200,000 species of BEETLES, and if only half of them are "biting ones," maybe you had better wear long sleeves on your next beetle hunt.

spider

One little "animal" which is not an insect, but an arachnid, is the SPIDER. If you're even seen a SPIDER web, you'll realize that SPIDERS are pretty good spinners, and that's where they got their name. The Middle English word "spithre" probably came from the Anglo-Saxon "spinthra" and "spinnan," which meant to spin. So the SPIDER might be called a spinning machine.

tarantula

TARANTULAS, commonly found in the city of Taranto, Italy, were believed to have caused a disease known as "tarantism" whenever they bit any of the citizens of Taranto. It was thought that a cure for the TARANTULA'S bite, or tarantism, was a fast, whirling dance which the people of Taranto named a "tarantella," a dance which fascinated the composers Chopin and Liszt so much that they wrote music for it.

tadpole

The TADPOLE is a young larva that plans to be a frog or toad when it grows up. TADPOLES seem to be frogs or toads which are all head, and that's how they got their name. In the Middle English language, "tade" and "tadde" were the words for toad, and "pol" was the word for head. By combining the words for "toad-head" we get the word TADPOLE.

turtle

Swimming around near the tadpole, you might see a TURTLE, a reptile which can be found on land or in water, but which is named for a bird. The word TURTLE comes from the Latin word "turtur," which came from the echoic sound of cooing made by certain wild doves known as turtledoves.

lobster

A creature which gets its name from a spider and a locust is the LOBSTER, that shellfish with five pairs of legs. The Latin word "locusta," meaning locust or lobster, was related to the Anglo-Saxon "loppe," meaning spider, and "loppestre," which in turn became the Middle English "lobstere," and finally LOBSTER, the spider of the sea.

porpoise

High above the lobster in both intelligence and speed is the PORPOISE. The word comes from the Middle English "porpoys," which came from the Old French "porpois," and was a shortening of the Latin words "porcus piscis," meaning pig fish. Evidently PORPOISES got their name from their "piglike" appearance in the water. The word PORPOISE is related to porcelain, which comes from "porcella," meaning little pig, and porcupine, which means a spiny little pig.

penguin

Another creature found in or near the ocean is the PENGUIN, which seems to have been named by Welsh fishermen. They combined the Welsh word "pen," which means head, with the Welsh word "gwyn," meaning white, thereby naming the PENGUIN for its "white head." The only trouble is that PENGUINS' heads are black, which means that those fishermen must have had some other bird in mind.

pigeon

PIGEON is another bird and another word which happens to be echoic. From the Lower Latin words "pipire" and "pipionis," which means the sound of peeping, to the Old French "pijon" and Middle English "pyjon," we get PIGEON, a peeping, chirping dove.

squirrel

Sometimes where we see pigeons we see SQUIRRELS, or at least the shadow of a SQUIRREL'S tail. The Greek word "skiouros" is made up of two other Greek words, "skia," meaning a shadow, and "oura," meaning tail. "Skiouros" became the Latin word "sciurus," the Lower Latin "sciuriolus," the Old French "esquirel," and the Middle English "squirel," all of which meant shadow tail.

Fido

Last but not the least of our words about the animal world is faithful FIDO, and faithful is exactly what his name means. FIDO probably comes from the Italian word "fido," meaning trusty, and goes back to the Latin "fidus," which means faithful. When we refer to a hi-fi radio set, we mean a set with high fidelity, or faithful sound. When you visit Old Faithful in the American West, perhaps you had better not call it Old Fido, even though it means that.

WHY IS HE BARKING AT THE GEYSER?

BECAUSE IT'S HIS BROTHER.

arf

Words About Other Things

Fahrenheit

One word we use which came from a person's name is FAHRENHEIT. Mr. Gabriel Daniel Fahrenheit was a German physicist. In 1714, he devised the temperature scale on which the freezing point of water is 32 degrees and the boiling point 212 degrees. People were so happy that they named it the FAHRENHEIT scale.

poinsettia

Another word which came from a person's name is the plant we often see at Christmastime, the POINSETTIA. It was named for Mr. Joel R. Poinsett, an ambassador to Mexico, who brought the plant to the United States. The POINSETTIA plant is one of the spurge plants, which include rubber trees and the plants which give us castor oil, tapioca, and Mexican jumping beans.

December

Christmas and poinsettia plants mean DECEMBER, the twelfth month of year. Yet the word DECEMBER refers to the "tenth month." What appears to be an error is not but is related to the early Roman calendar, which had only ten months, starting with March and finishing with DECEMBER. DECEMBER comes from the Latin word "decem,"

meaning ten, which also gives us the word decade, a period of ten years, and the decimal system, a system based on the number ten.

chimney

When you hang your Christmas stocking by the CHIMNEY, you'll be hanging it by a word which has meant oven, furnace, flue, hearth, and a room with a fireplace. CHIMNEY comes from the Greek "kaminos" meaning oven or fireplace, which became the Latin "caminus," the Old French "cheminée," the Middle English "chimenee," and finally our word CHIMNEY.

tattoo

One word with two meanings and two origins but one spelling is the word TATTOO. TATTOO, meaning to mark the skin with designs, comes from the Tahitian word "tatu," and is a lengthening of their word "ta," which means to paint or mark. The word TATTOO, meaning a bugle call or drumbeat calling soldiers back to their quarters, comes from the Dutch "tap-toe," "tap" being faucet, and "toe," related to the German "zu," meaning shut or to close. Telling soldiers that the "tap was being shut," or the barrooms were closing, was the meaning of the second word TATTOO.

candle

Long ago when people wanted to buy CANDLES, they went to a person called a chandler, meaning candle dealer and eventually just dealer. Variations of the word CANDLE come from the Latin word "candere," meaning to shine, the Latin word "candela," meaning a light or torch, and the Anglo-Saxon and Middle English word "candel," which means CANDLE.

42

laser

One word that's been shortened right down to its initials is the word LASER. It comes from the first letter of the key words in the phrase "*L*ight *A*mplification by *S*timulated *E*mission of *R*adiation." By using the initials or first few letters of several words to form a new word, we are creating an "acronym."

radar

Another word which is an acronym, and a palindrome as well, is the word RADAR. The word RADAR comes from "*R*adio *D*etecting *A*nd *R*anging," and is an acronym made up of letters from that phrase. It is a palindrome, a word which comes from the Greek words "palin," meaning again, and "dramein," meaning to run, because it reads the same backward or forward. The words civic, madam, noon, tot, dad, pop, mom, toot, and sis are palindromes.

cartoon

Most people would guess that when cartoonists start to draw a CARTOON, they start with a large piece of paper, or card, and that's how the word CARTOON started too. The Italian word "cartone," which comes from the French word "carton," both come from the Late Latin "carta," meaning card. Card, chart, and Magna Carta, which means "great charter," are all related to the word CARTOON.

cradle

If you want to describe a CRADLE to someone, you might say it looks like a little basket. You won't be wrong, since that's where the word CRADLE comes from. The Old High German word "kratto" meant basket, and became the Anglo-Saxon word "cradol" and the Middle English "cradel," meaning little basket. From "cradel" to the English word CRADLE was only a slight change.

pillow

Speaking of cradles reminds us of sleeping on something soft like a PILLOW. Yet the word PILLOW probably started out meaning a block of wood or short log. The Middle English "pilwe" and Middle Latin "pulvinus" both came from the Latin "puluinus," meaning PILLOW. "Puluinus" possibly came from the ancient Hittite word "pulpule," meaning a kind of tree, or the Indo-European word "pul," which meant a short log, something that doesn't seem like a very good PILLOW.

alarm

There is probably nothing that will awaken a sleeper more than the ringing of the clock's ALARM. But the original meaning of that word was a "a sudden warning of danger," not just something to keep us from sleeping late. The word ALARM comes from the Italian "all'arme," meaning "to arms!", and the Old French and Middle English "alarme," which in early days were urgent calls to arms.

spatula

Something which belongs in the kitchen instead of the bedroom is the SPATULA. This tool, so helpful for flipping flapjacks, took its name from its shape. It went from the Greek "spathe" to the Latin "spata," which was a broad-bladed sword, similar to a spade. From "spata" to the diminutive SPATULA, meaning "small" sword or blade, the word came to mean the kitchen implement we use for eggs.

yellow

The eggs we turn with the spatula, or at least the yolks, are very closely related to the next word, YELLOW. The Indo-European word "ghel," meaning to shine or glitter, was related to the words gold and YELLOW. That led to the German "gelb" and the Anglo-Saxon "geolu." Then the word entered the Middle English language as "yelwe," became "yelow" and finally YELLOW. Meanwhile the word for egg yolk had become the Anglo-Saxon "geolca," the Middle English "yolke," until it became yolk, the golden YELLOW part of the egg we flip.

Frisbee

Speaking of flipping brings up the word FRISBEE, the toy shaped like a pie plate. It seems that in the 1920s, someone took a pie plate from the Frisbie bakery in Bridgeport, Connecticut, and by turning it upside down was able to flip it quite far. Flipping Mrs. Frisbie's pie plates became a popular new sport or game with local college students. It became more popular when plastic FRISBEES were manufactured and sold in 1957. The next time you flip a FRISBEE, you'll be flipping a toy that started as a pie plate in a Bridgeport bakery and entered the English language as a new word.

goodbye

Now for the last word of 101 More Words and How They Began. Somehow it seems suitable to choose the word GOODBYE. This familiar form of farewell comes from the contraction, or shortened form, of the English phrase "God be with you." From "God be with you" to "God be wi'ye" to "god bw'ye" to "god bwye," that phrase became shortened from four words to the one word we know so well, GOODBYE.

And so, we've talked about another 101 words and how they began. One hundred and one is a very small number of words when we realize that most standard dictionaries contain over 20,000 entries. Not many people know and use all those 20,000 words, but the more words we know the better we will be able to express ourselves.

There are some people who add a word a day to their vocabularies in an interesting way. Each day they open a dictionary and start at the beginning. When they come to a word they have never seen before, they study it, learn how to pronounce it, and use the new word at least once in conversation that day. The next day they learn another new word in the same way. At the end of the year they have added 365 new words to their vocabularies.

46

Of the thousands and thousands of words, some can make you happy, some can make you sad, and some can even make you hungry. Words can be written, lettered, or typed. They can be carved in stone or written in the sand. They can be thought, whispered, spoken, or yelled. Words can be used for games and puzzles and stories long after the lights are out and other games and puzzles and stories are put away.

As someone once said, words are even better than toys; they don't break, they just about never wear out, they can be used over and over again, they come in all types and sizes and for all ages. You don't need batteries to use them, you don't have to put them away when you're through playing with them, and they're so very, very inexpensive.